A COMPLETE INTRODUCTION TO MOUNTAIN BIKING

MTB TIPS FOR BEGINNERS: TECHNIQUES, MAINTENANCE, SAFETY AND MORE!

SAM FURY

Illustrated by
NEIL GERMIO

WARNINGS AND DISCLAIMERS

The information in this publication is made public for reference only.

Neither the author, publisher, nor anyone else involved in the production of this publication is responsible for how the reader uses the information or the result of his/her actions.

CONTENTS

THANKS FOR YOUR PURCHASE

Did you know you can get FREE chapters of any SF Nonfiction Book you want?

https://www.SFNonfictionBooks.com/Free-Chapters

You will also be among the first to know of FREE review copies, discount offers, bonus content, and more.

Go to:

https://www.SFNonfictionBooks.com/Free-Chapters

Thanks again for your support.

INTRODUCTION

Mountain biking, an off-road form of cycling, is an extremely popular two-wheeled sport. This is because it is versatile.

It is accessible to all ages, fitness levels, and skill levels. It can also be done anywhere - on hillsides or on a plateau.

Bike riding is a fun way to connect with nature and exercise. Mountain bikes differ from road bikes in the following ways:

- The tires are wider and have rugged treads for stability and durability in off-road terrain
- The upright position allows for better views while cycling
- Some bikes are equipped with suspension systems to reduce shock while riding

Mountain biking can be enjoyed in many different ways, and you don't even have to be in the mountains to do it. You can ride on wide, flowing logging roads or challenge yourself on technical single tracks.

Mountain Bike VS Road Bike

Mountain Bike

Mountain bikes are heavier, bigger, and equipped with thick, durable tires to handle the off-road challenges.

Road Bikes

Road bikes are fast, lightweight, and designed to be used on roads and well-maintained trails.

Their aerodynamic design and thin, high-pressure tires help you to travel long distances with great speed.

Mountain Bike   **Road Bike**

ANATOMY OF A MOUNTAIN BIKE

Given below are different mountain bike parts that you must know as a beginner before you start your mountain biking journey.

Mountain Bike Parts

1. *Brake caliper*

Front and rear discs are equipped with brake calipers attached to the levers by brake lines. The brake lines press against opposing pistons in the calipers, which force the brake pads inward to make contact with the disc. As a result, the bike slows down because of the friction.

2. *Brake disc*

Disc brakes slow or stop your bike using a hydraulic or cable-actuated caliper to force pads over a rotor.

3. *Brake lever*

The brake lever actuates the bike's brake.

4. *Cassette*

Cassettes are stacks of sprockets integrated with the rear derailleur of the mountain bike.

5. *Chain*

Power is transferred from the front to the rear sprockets with the help of a chain made up of interconnected plates, pins, and rollers.

6. *Chainring*

Front gears are called chainrings, or cranksets. Generally, the crank arms and the gears are referred to as the 'crankset' or the 'chainset' together. Generally, cranksets have either two (referred to as double or 2x), or three (referred to as triple or 3x) chainrings. The smallest chainring on the crankset lies closest to the frame. Pedaling is easier when the chainring is smaller.

7. *Chainstay*

A chainstay is the pair of tubes that run from the bottom bracket to the rear fork ends of a bicycle frame.

8. *Crank arm*

The crank arms of your mountain bike are an integral part of the drive assembly. You pedal power through the crank arms, which act as a connection between the pedal and the bottom bracket. By using a crank arm, part of the crankset, you can apply force to the pedal, which is transmitted via the crank arm to the forward gears, which drive the chain on the bicycle.

9. *Down tube*

The down tube is a tube running from the head tube to the bottom bracket of the bike's frame.

10. *Fork arm*

It attaches the frame of the bike to the front wheel and handlebars and allows you to steer the bike using the steerer tube.

11. *Fork crown*

The fork crown is the support that holds the stanchions of a fork in place. The fork's fork blades meet at this point below the steerer tube. Mountain bikes typically have single crown forks. Downhill bikes are more frequently equipped with dual-crown forks, which are stiffer and more suitable for longer travel bikes, typically, downhill bikes.

12. *Fork dropout hub*

The fork dropout hub is the slot that sits in the rear axle of a mountain bike that lets you remove the wheel without removing or derailing the chain. It is the place where the axle of a bicycle wheel is attached to the bicycle frame or fork.

13. *Fork slider*

With fork sliders, the forks are protected from mild low sides and tipovers, which could topple the bike at a weird angle and damage the forks. The purpose of these sliders is to prevent damage to the fork bottom (front suspension), the brake calipers, and the axle nut of the bike.

14. *Fork stanchion*

Stanchions are parts of the fork that slide into the lowers. Different fork types have different stanchion diameters. The bigger the stanchion diameter, the stiffer the fork, but the heavier it becomes. This is why downhill forks typically have the largest stanchion diameters, and cross country forks have the smallest.

15. *Front derailleur*

The derailleur is the component that allows a bicycle to change gear by moving the chain from sprocket to sprocket. The bike has two derailleurs, one at the rear and one at the front.

The chain moves between three front sprockets with the help of the front derailleur. The front derailleur, in contrast to the rear derailleur, moves the upper part of the chain, which is under tension while pedaling. Therefore, you must ease off the pedals in order to change the sprockets on the front.

16. *Grip*

A mountain bike grip is essentially a piece of rubber attached to your handlebars that you hold onto. One of the most commonly used designs is the lock-on design which consists of one or two clamps at each end.

17. *Headtube*

On a bicycle, the head tube is a portion of the tubular frame that contains the front fork steerer tube. The head tube holds the bearings that permit the steerer tube of the front fork to pivot independently.

18. *Monocoque*

A monocoque bike frame utilizes a single skin to handle forces and loads. When compared to body-on-frame construction, a monocoque construction will always perform better. A monocoque construction allows the floor pan to be placed much lower, lowering the bike's center of gravity. This makes the bike more agile.

19. *Pedal*

Foot and crank arm are connected by a pedal. Generally, there are two types; one secures the foot using a mechanical clamp or cage, whereas the other does not provide any type of connection to lock the foot to the pedal.

20. *Rear dropout*

A rear dropout is where the hanger for the rear derailleur is attached to the frame. On the rear portion of a bike frame, the rear dropout is the point where the chainstay joins with the seat stay (the confluence).

21. *Rear shock*

There are two main types of mountain bikes: hardtails and full suspensions. When going downhill or over obstacles, a full-suspension bike has a rear shock or suspension to enhance comfort and control.

22. *Rim*

The rim is the part of a wheel attached to which the tire is mounted, and it often functions as a braking mechanism.

23. *Saddle*

A saddle is a seat on a bike. Various types of saddles are available, ranging from those that are heavily padded to those that are sleeker and more race-oriented.

24. *Saddle clamp*

The saddle clamps, also referred to as pipe saddles, are used in temporary or permanent installations for adding branch lines to piping systems.

25. *Saddle rail*

The rails of a saddle provide the connection between the saddle and the rest of the bike. A strip of leather runs along the underside of the saddle from the nose to the back. A saddle generally contains two parallel rails to which the seat post is attached, but designs can vary from one to four rails.

26. *Seat collar*

Seat collars are circular metal collars attached to the top of the seat tube, and their job is to firmly clamp down on that tube in order to prevent the saddle from rotating during riding or preventing the post from sinking into the frame.

27. *Seat post*

A seat post is a tube attached to the bicycle frame, which connects to the saddle where you sit. It is useful because it allows for adjustment.

This allows the same frame to accommodate riders of different sizes or be customized for different riding styles or terrains.

28. *Seat stay*

The seat tube is connected to the rear dropout by the seat stay. A typical bike frame uses two parallel tubes that join above the rear wheel. Additionally, this is where the rear brake caliper is attached to the frame.

29. *Seat tube*

In a bike frame, a seat tube is a typically vertical tube that runs from the seat to the bottom bracket.

30. *Shift lever*

Bicycle shifters, gear shifters, or gear levers are used to select gear ratios and control gearing mechanisms. Typically, they function either with a derailleur mechanism or with an internal gear mechanism located within the hub.

31. *Tire*

Tires are ring-shaped parts that surround a wheel's rim to transmit the bike's load from the axle to the wheel and to provide traction when the wheel rolls over uneven surfaces. Pneumatically inflated tires, such as those used for mountain bikes, provide flexibility and absorb shock as the tire rolls over rough terrain.

Related Chapters:

- Types of Mountain Bikes

MOUNTAIN BIKING TRAILS

Although you might start out on trails that are relatively flat and smooth, your ability to navigate obstacles will develop as you gain experience. A mountain biking trail is usually marked by your skill level (beginner, intermediate, expert, and double expert) and is maintained accordingly as well.

Singletrack

A singletrack trail, the most commonly encountered trail type, ranges in width from a little wider than your shoulder to a narrow enough track for two bikes to pass in a straight line.

Singletrack trails are often one-way and wind their way through the most scenic terrain the area has to offer.

Doubletrack

A doubletrack trail is normally twice as wide (or more) as a typical singletrack trail, allowing two bikes to be ridden together. A double-track trail is often made from two single tracks created by the tires of vehicles on old logging roads, fire roads, or power line roads.

Most doubletrack trails are flatter and less technical than singletrack trails.

Mountain Bike Terrain Parks

The number of mountain bike terrain parks is growing everywhere, from jump-and-pump tracks under overpasses to trails accessible by lift at ski resorts.

There are berms, banked corners, and hairy switchbacks downhill as well as halfpipes, jumps of various sizes, and elevated bridges.

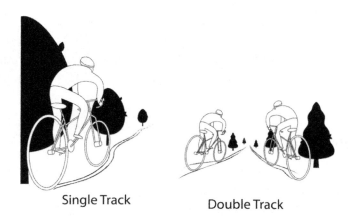

Single Track   Double Track

MOUNTAIN BIKING STYLES

To help you determine what type of bike is right for you, many bike manufacturers categorize their bikes according to the following mountain biking styles.

Trail

This is arguably the most popular style of mountain biking since it is not associated with a specific form of racing. You're more likely to enjoy this style of riding if you want to meet up with friends at a local trailhead and ride a mixture of climbs and descents. In this category, bikes emphasize fun, efficiency, and weight at the same time.

Cross-country

Cross-country involves riding fast and having strong climbing skills. The distances covered range from a few miles to more than 25 miles, and the bikes tend to be lightweight and efficient. If you're thinking about getting competitive or would prefer a faster ride for your local trails, these are great.

Enduro/all-mountain

The all-mountain/enduro riding style is akin to trail riding on steroids, with up-and-down climbs, long descents, and technical terrain both man-made and natural. A well-designed all-mountain/enduro bike will perform well on steep descents, while at the same time being light and nimble enough to climb.

Enduro is a racing world term that describes a competition with timed downhill stages and untimed uphill stages. The winner is the person with the fastest total downhill time. With the popularity of enduro riding, the term has become interchangeable with all-mountain, regardless of whether you race.

Downhill/park

Lift-serviced bike parks are most commonly used for this type of riding (usually during warmer months at ski resorts). The bikes you ride are big, and tough, and you wear full-face helmets and armor. There are fewer gears and stronger components on these bikes, and their suspension travel is longer (the amount of movement). You can use all this to master jumps, rock gardens, berms, and wooden ladders. You don't have to pedal much since you're on a continuous descent, but you still get a serious workout as you're always adjusting to the fast-approaching terrain.

Fat-tire-biking

If you were a kid, you probably dreamed of having a bike with giant tires that could handle whatever you threw at it.

Fat-tire bikes have tires that are at least 3.7 inches wide. Some are as wide as 5 inches. These bikes provide great traction in snow and sand. There are many conditions for fat-tire biking, and it's been a fast-growing part of all-season trail riding. Fat-tire bikes are very forgiving on rough terrain, which is why they are a great choice for beginner mountain bikers.

TYPES OF MOUNTAIN BIKES

The type of bike you ride depends on where you intend to ride. There are two key factors that determine what type of terrain the bike can ride: suspension type and wheel diameter. When it comes to suspension types and wheel diameters, you have a wealth of options (expressed by terms like 26, 27.5 (650b), and 29ers).

Suspension Type

Rigid

Unlike most other types of mountain bikes, rigid mountain bikes have no suspension. Despite their rigidity, many fat-tire bikes offer enough squish to absorb bumps in the trail, thanks to their wide tires and low tire pressure.

Hardtail

There is a suspension fork in the front of these bikes to help absorb impacts on the front wheel, but there is no suspension in the rear, thus the term hardtail. A hardtail bike is often more affordable and has fewer moving parts than a full-suspension bike (which often means less maintenance). Hardtails often have the ability to lock out their front forks for times when a rigid bike is preferred.

Cross-country riders generally prefer hardtails because they allow more direct power transfer from the pedal stroke to the rear tire. Hardtails are also at home on all-mountain trails, and their lower costs and easier maintenance make them a good option for everything but downhill trails that require lift service.

Full suspension

The basic idea behind full-suspension bikes is that the forks and shocks absorb the impacts of the trail. The rider will experience less impact, increase traction, and have a more comfortable experience.

If you have a full-suspension bike, it can take a lot of bumps and chatter, but if you are climbing uphill, the bike may "bob" a bit and you will lose some power transfer. Most full-suspension rigs offer the option to lock out the rear suspension to improve power transfer and climbing efficiency.

When compared to cross-country and all-mountain bikes, downhill bikes tend to have a lot of travel, or movement in the suspension. Some bikes feature up to eight inches of travel in front and rear.

Wheel Size

24 inch

Kids' mountain bikes typically have 24-inch wheels. This is to accommodate their shorter legs. They are generally less expensive versions of adult bicycles with simpler components. It is generally recommended for kids ages 10 to 13, but it really depends on the size of the child. Littler/younger children can even start biking with 20-inch wheels.

26 inch

Back in the day, all mountain bikes had 26-inch wheels. There is still a demand for this wheel size due to its responsiveness and maneuverability, however, if you walk into a bike shop asking for mountain bikes, you're likely to hear, "26 inches, 27.5 inches, or 29 inches?"

27.5 inch (650b)

This middle ground between 26 and 29-inch wheels offers the best of both worlds, rolling over terrain with less effort than 26-inch wheels while offering more maneuverability than 29-inch wheels. The wheel size can be found on both hardtails and full-suspension rigs, just like 29ers.

29ers

Typically, 29-inch wheels make these bikes heavier and more difficult to accelerate, but once you are moving you can conquer much more terrain than you could on a 26-inch wheel bike. Most of them are extremely grippable, and they have a high "attack angle", which makes them easier to roll over trail obstacles. Cross-country riders like these bikes a lot. You can get 29ers with either a hardtail or a full-suspension rig.

HOW TO CHOOSE A MOUNTAIN BIKE

Whether you're new to MTB or a road rider wanting to hit the dirt and go off-road, it helps to know what to look for when choosing a mountain bike.

1. Make sure you get the right size

It's important to start with the right frame size, then everything else will fall into place. However, do not rely on stated sizes. Although many companies are replacing the increasingly inaccurate size scales with small, medium, and large, (seat tubes are shrinking as frames grow), there is no standard definition of what is large. For example, one brand's medium can be another's large.

You should instead ensure that your bike fits you properly. Consider (and compare) the reach (distance from the saddle to handlebars) and stack measures (center of the crank to mid-head tube distance) measurements, and be open to going longer than with a road bike. Having a long front triangle puts the axle further forward, allowing you to weigh it (for grip) without worrying that you'll fall over the bars on your first impact. Additionally, having a long front triangle makes climbing easier by keeping the front wheel planted.

If you go too long, you won't have sufficient clearance for a standover. A couple of centimeters is all you need. If your seat tube is short, you will have a good standover and the most maneuvering room. However, make sure that you have enough pedaling height without overextending the seat post. 29er bikes have taller fronts, and you can considerably alter your riding position with different stems, bars, and seat posts.

2. Selecting a wheel size

We have settled on a simple, binary choice of 27.5 inches (650b, downhill, and aggressive trail) or 29 inches (trail and XC). Yet the proliferation of wide-rimmed plus sizes and the recent fad for down-hill wheels of 29 inches are muddying the waters.

Over time, 29ers that are stiff, light, and strong(ish) will become more common, along with appropriate tires and frames. For now, the choice is basically the same: choose bigger rims for long rides, or smaller, stronger rims for crushing trails. The crusher fine trail, or a crushing trail, combines a natural feel with a durable surface (rather than concrete or asphalt). With a natural gravel-like surface, this path has the feel of a trail rather than a hard surfaced path and blends well with primitive surroundings. On hardtails, plus sizes are great, but they are sensitive to tire pressure and their long-term viability is a bit questionable.

3. Select a hardtail or full suspension (full-suss) bike

The cost of the rear shock, bearings, linkages and the extra manu-facturing complications that go into full suspension are high. A hardtail is likely to have better parts specifications than a full-suss bike at the same price. It will require less maintenance and be less likely to break down.

In contrast, full-suss bikes are now more advanced than ever, so they can still be an advantage. There's certainly no need to dismiss either, but you shouldn't think that you have to 'learn' on a hardtail before getting your own 'big bike' - that's a myth. Whichever you prefer is up to you.

4. Try not to obsess about weight

While weight is an important factor, strength tends to matter more off-road. The flimsy bike has no place when you are constantly being grabbed by random rocks, ruts, and roots. With inaccurate steering, cornering, and lack of confidence, your speed also decreases. A few extra pounds are better than smashing into the hedge and losing your bike.

5.   Don't fall for flashy trinkets

You should never be fooled by a nice rear mech (derailleur). They often show higher specifications than what the bike actually has to make the bike more appealing. The mech is important, but so is the shifter and crankset – even the chainrings play a role. If you plan to upgrade in the future, you should consider lower-spec components that are heavier and more rudimentary.

6.   Choose quality suspensions, not quantity

Check out the reviews of the forks and shocks (on the full suspension) on the bike you're looking at, and use the manufacturer's website to get the exact model. Original equipment (OE) units will often have a different (often lower) specification than similar-looking aftermarket units. Any amount of extra travel won't make any difference if you have quality damping and a decent air spring.

7.   Choose a design that is future-proof

Check the diameters of the axles and spacing as well as the headset, bottom bracket, and even the seat post – you'll have trouble finding the increasingly popular dropper post (for altering saddle height as needed) that has the smallest diameter. Although internal routing for droppers is ideal, what internal gear cables and brake hoses gain in looks they can lose in noise and ease of maintenance.

SETTING UP THE BIKE BEFORE THE RIDE

Suspension

Set the suspension stiffness to your weight (this will usually be done at the shop). It is a key setting that you must do. For air suspension, you can buy an air pump and set the pressure yourself, but for a mountain bike beginner, it is better to have someone else do it. Ask your bike shop or a friend who rides a mountain bike. You may also be able to adjust other settings on your suspension depending on its quality. Rebound is the most common one - the speed at which the shock returns to its initial state following compression. As a beginner, you should just ask at the shop for these to be set in a neutral state for your weight.

Tire Pressure

Make sure the tire pressure is correct. The tire pressure on a mountain bike should be between 25 and 35 psi. Thinner tires require higher pressure while wider tires need lower pressure. Tires usually have the recommended maximum and minimum pressure listed on the side. After some time, you will be able to determine what tire pressure you need based on your weight, riding style, and the trails you ride. When going up, some mountain bikers also pump up their tires to reduce rolling resistance. When going down, they let the air out for better traction.

Pedals

Whenever you buy a decent-quality mountain bike, it always comes without proper pedals. It may have some cheap plastic pedals, but you should not use them to ride your bike. This is probably because pedals are a personal choice. A pedal is one of three points of contact between you and your bike (grips, pedals, seat) which is especially important when riding downhill.

So what's so important to know about pedals?

Well, for starters, if you don't buy them with your bike, you won't be able to ride it!

There are two types of pedals for mountain bikes: clipless pedals and flat pedals.

Clipless pedals: Clipless pedals secure your foot to the pedal so it does not move. Because it remains in the same position, you can control your bike better. Their downside is that you have to get used to them in order to clip out when you need to get off the bike. That can be difficult. You'll need pedals and special shoes to use this system. The use of clipless pedals on a mountain bike is not recommended for beginners, especially on technical trails.

In fact, early all mountain bike riders use flat pedals.

Flat pedals (flats): Flat pedals are not attached to your feet; you just stand on them. Using metal pins that point out of the flat pedals, flat pedals prevent your foot from slipping and moving around. When combined with mtb shoes that have strong rubber soles with lots of grips, pins will keep your foot in place. However, regular shoes can also be used with flats.

The downside is that you may stand on them incorrectly since your feet are not attached (normally, the balls of your feet should be in the middle of the pedal). Worse still, you may slip off and hit the pins on your shin. However, when you are learning, you can step off your bike whenever you want - and you will be doing this a lot. Eventually, you may step down in more difficult situations, either purposefully or unintentionally.

There is a problem with clipless pedals in that, in critical situations, you will have to disconnect from them. For example, when you are in a difficult place on a trail, when you are losing your balance, and when you have to step off quickly. If you don't, you may crash. Nevertheless, riding clipless or flats depends on individual preference.

Remember that a lighter pedal is better and more expensive.

Platform size, or the part of the pedal you stand on, depends on your foot size and your personal taste. Bigger pedals usually give you more confidence.

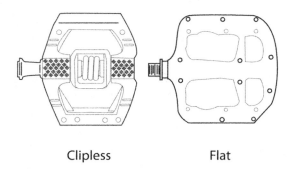

Clipless   Flat

MOUNTAIN BIKE MAINTENANCE

The maintenance of your bike will ensure the longevity of the machine and regular maintenance will build your trust in it. As a beginner, a mountain bike can seem intimidating, but there are many checks and ways of maintaining your bike that are both simple and quick.

Checks To Do

Ideally, you should check your bike before each and every ride. The routine will become instinctive after a while, but to begin, you must remember a few areas to check for wear and damage:

- Chain: Oil the chain if it is brown and rusted. If one or more of the links are stuck, the chain needs to be replaced before further damage occurs.
- Tires: A quick squeeze of each tire prevents you from riding out with a slow puncture already in place.
- Wheels and discs: Rotate the front wheel of the bike by lifting it up. Repeat for the rear wheel. Both should spin freely and without any friction or noise coming from the discs.
- Suspension: When the suspension bounces, both front, and rear at the same time, it means something is wrong and you should investigate it further - take it in to be repaired. Even if you think everything was fine on your last ride, it is always a good idea to check. It is amazing what you can miss after a long ride.
- Test ride: Take the bike out for a quick spin and check for squeaks, creaks, or crunches. Make sure the gears are indexed correctly by moving up and down the range.

When you're done with this process, which should take no more than a minute if nothing is wrong, you'll be ready to enjoy your ride with the confidence that your bike is in good working condition.

Cleaning The Bike

A mountain bike is constantly subjected to mud and water – an obvious occupational risk – and it is built to withstand that punishment. It is important to keep in mind that bearings and other moving parts cannot tolerate mud and water for long. You might think cleaning your bike is easy, but if you follow these tips, your bike will last you a lot longer:

- Be quick: Do not worry about your hunger or cold after a ride; the sooner you start cleaning your bike, the easier it will be because the dirt and water will still be loose.
- Spray with water: Spray the entire bike with a low-pressure hose to make sure all dirt/mud is wet. Doing so will make things much easier afterward.
- Cleaning agent: A high-quality bike cleaning spray helps dislodge dirt from every nook and cranny of the bike. These products all contain strong chemicals, so don't leave them on for too long or your paintwork will be dull. You should not use washing liquid on brake pads or grease as it can contaminate them.
- Loosen the dirt: If you have applied a bike cleaner, use a brush to loosen the dirt and to create foam.
- Spray: Spray the bike clean and repeat the procedure if necessary. Check the gears, saddle, and steerer tube for mud or debris.
- Buff and lubricate: Using a dry, clean cloth, buff the bike and make sure there are no watermarks left behind. Using the cloth, pat the chain dry and then apply some quality lube, making sure not to touch the rear disc where you apply it. As you apply the lube to the chain at the rear

derailleur, lean the bike up against a wall and spin the pedals backward.

Clean bikes are happy bikes, and you will enjoy riding a functional bike that has been well taken care of each time you leave the house. You should clean your bike as soon as you get home from riding it since it takes no more than 5 minutes. If you leave it until the mud goes hard, it will take much longer.

After-ride Checks

After cleaning and lubricating your bike, you may want to consider performing several after-ride checks. It is a good idea to include these in a weekly schedule to ensure the safety of your bike and its longevity:

- The bolt check: Make sure all the bolts on the bike are tightened, from the handlebars to the rear derailleur. Bolts can easily come loose on a ride, so check them fairly frequently.
- Wheels: Make sure that your wheels' quick releases or bolts are straight and tight after every ride.
- Spoke tension: You can quickly determine the spoke tension by simply pinging the spokes. As you hear the pitch change, feel the tension in the spokes one pair at a time.
- Air pressures: Since air suspension loses pressure over time, check the PSI of the front and rear units every five rides.
- Creaks: Bounce on the bike a little while holding the handlebars and pedals and listen for creaks. A common cause of creaks is dry bolt threads; as soon as you locate the creak, remove the bolts (i.e. the four bolts that hold the handlebars in place) and clean the threads. Ensure the bolts are replaced and tightened and, if the creaking still occurs, seek advice -- it could indicate a hidden hairline crack or faulty bearings.

Additionally, a full strip-down of the bike twice a month is worthwhile. Visit your local bike shop for this. A full strip-down of the bike will clear your bottom bracket and hubs of any hidden mud, clean and lubricate all bearings and threads, tighten everything to the correct torque settings, and thoroughly clean the drivetrain. You can expect your bike to run like new and last much longer.

Tuning The Gears

Every now and then, your gears will go out of sync due to cable stretch, constant rattling, and the general punishment your mountain bike takes. You shouldn't worry about this and a minute of tuning up should fix the issues.

Step 1 - Alignment

A bike shop will need to straighten or replace the rear derailleur if the hanger (that connects it to the frame) is bent or twisted. Make sure the hanger and derailleur of the gears are straight when looking from the rear.

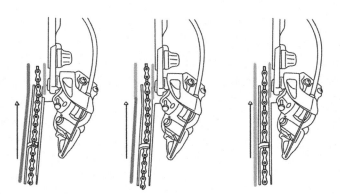

Step 2 - Low and High

An adjustable high-low point on the derailleur determines where the outermost gear sits. As a result, when on the top or bottom gear, the chain and sprocket should be directly lined up with the derailleur.

For setting the rear gears:

- Start with the smallest sprocket and then look down the derailleur's length from behind. Derailleurs should have jockey wheels lined up exactly with sprockets.
- If they do not, turn the cross-head screwdriver bolt marked 'high' and the derailleur will be put in place.

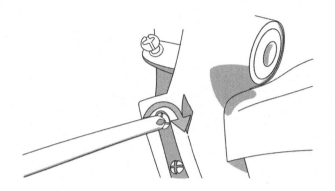

- This applies to the low gears and the front mech, which should run without rubbing from the chain as you turn the pedals.

Step 3 - Cable

Providing the high and low gears are set and everything is straight, the cable is usually the most common factor that affects the gear's performance.

To determine the problem, perform the following checks:

- Is it rusted? If the cable is rusty, or muddy, it will be unable to move freely through the outer housing. You can spray some oil through the housing to help it move freely. Your cable probably needs to be replaced if it won't move freely.

- It will also be difficult for the cable to move freely if it's kinked anywhere, so you will have difficulty switching from 1st to 8/9th gear. If there is a kink in the cable, you will need to buy a new one.

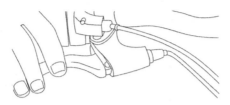

- Check the smallest sprocket for cable tension; the cable should not be loaded by the shifter. Press on the exposed piece of the inner cable near the derailleur after dropping the bike into the smallest sprocket. It should not be slack. Pull a little more cable through the derailleur until it is taught. If it's still loose, unbolt the bolt that holds it in place.
- A barrel adjuster is used to fine-tune the gears. It is the small, black plastic dials on both ends of the cable: both on the derailleur and on the gear shifter. The cable will be put under more tension by twisting these black plastic dials anti-clockwise, which will cause the drive train to run more smoothly.

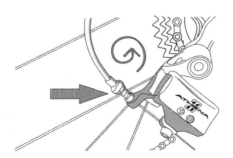

Re-aligning Brakes

When your disc brakes are out of alignment, they can lead to a number of issues, such as noises/squeals and a shortened lifespan for the brake pads. This is not a major problem, and the brake caliper and its fittings are likely to suffer from it simply because of the enormous forces they have to deal with.

For re-aligning a brake:

- Start by removing the two bolts holding the caliper in place (that attach to the frame/forks). It should be loose but not completely detached.
- Pull the brake lever so that the brake pads clamp the disc.
- Make sure that the brake caliper is on the disc while pulling the brake lever in.
- Retighten the two bolts and then relax the brake lever.

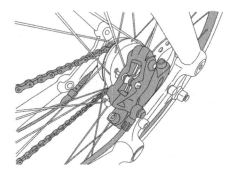

The disc should now be centered within the brake pads; the clamping action while the caliper was loose will help to do this. Make sure there is no rubbing on the wheel, and if there is, repeat the process. If there is still noise/rubbing, check that the disc is not bent.

Frame Safety Checks

You should inspect the bike's frame every five or so rides. Additionally, check the rims (the wheels) for cracks and anything out of the ordinary. Handlebar cracks must be treated very carefully, and any noise should be addressed immediately.

Keep an eye out for hairline cracks in the welds at the tubes' joints. Ideally, you want to catch frame faults before a complete failure can occur, which could result in injury. There is a limit to how well mountain bikes can endure punishment; therefore, frame failure can occur; however, most major manufacturers provide warranty services.

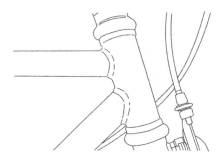

Maintenance Tips To Keep In Mind

- With a mountain bike, maintenance should be done more frequently than with a road bike - before each ride, mountain bikers should check and maintain their bikes properly.
- The demands on a mountain bike are higher. A jump or impact can crack the frame or damage the tire rims, and a steep, fast descent can quickly wear out the brake pads.
- Adjust the brakes to stop your bike properly as you descend. Common brake problems include brake cable stretching, worn brake pads, and brakes that are out of alignment.
- Look for cracks or damaged areas on the frame.
- The front and rear axles should be tight.
- The headset and stem should be secure with no looseness.

- Make sure your tires are in proper condition with no cuts or tears in the sidewall.
- Ideally, a bike's handlebars and grips should be tight and not spin.
- Fasten the seat and the seat post firmly.
- The chain and chainset will last longer if you regularly apply oil to them.

You need to know your bike and understand when/which gears cause you trouble. It's best if you take any problems to a local bike shop if you can't fix them yourself. It's better to be safe than sorry!

BASIC REPAIRS

The wear and tear on your bike over time, especially if you enjoy riding rough terrain, can quickly add up in maintenance costs. Learning how to do some basic repairs yourself can save you some money. Additionally, this will help you if you're stranded in the middle of nowhere with no bike shop in sight in case of an emergency.

Wrapping

When it comes to a good ride, comfort is essential and a poor grip will throw you off your game. The rubber on your handlebar tapes can get soiled a number of times over a few days from rain, mud, sand, or snow, making them rough or slick and hard to hold onto. The process of removing and replacing the tape is straightforward and every biker should know how to do it. Having a tape kit handy makes the process much easier. They can also include scissors, which, depending on how sticky your last wrap was, might be essential.

Wrap clockwise under the handlebar and toward the center where the two sides meet. Be sure to overlap your wrapping as you go to prevent gaps. If you want a little extra security, wrap it twice and secure it with electric tape.

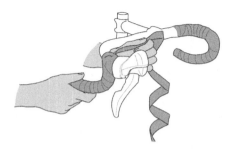

Remove the old tape and clean any sticky residue.

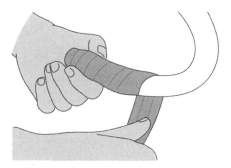

Start by wrapping the bars from the bottom. Keep even tension on the tape.

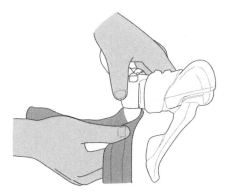

Place the extra bar piece on the levers.

Cut the end of the tape at an angle to get a neat finish.

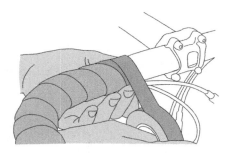

Secure the wrap with an electric tape.

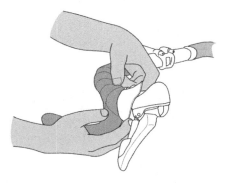

Make sure to replace the cover of the hoods.

Chain Repair

Of all the different components of a bicycle, the chain is the one that carries the most weight. It ensures everything works smoothly and is also one of the first parts to wear out when overused.

Regularly check the number of teeth exposed under the chainring to prevent a surprise breakdown. If you need to remove parts of the link, keep a chain breaker and/or multi-tool on hand.

As each brand has its own unique way of designing and repairing its products, it's important to study your manual and memorize it.

Choose a tool that will work in every situation.

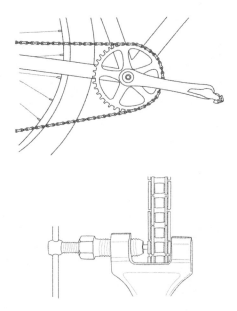

Fixing A Flat Tire

A flat tire ends any ride quickly. Unless you don't mind having a spare on your back while you ride, changing the entire tire on the trail is probably not an option, but something as small as a puncture is easy to fix.

If you keep a spare tube on hand and brush up on your tire removal skills, you'll be able to do it regardless of your skill level.

There are plenty of tools available to help you take off the tire, but in most cases, you can simply use your ingenuity and elbow grease to get the job done.

Remember to let out the remaining air from the tire before you begin your repair and, after you remove the old tube and install the new one, make sure to close the quick-release valve.

How To Repair A Flat Tire

1. *Remove the Wheel*

If you have rim brakes, you will need to release them.

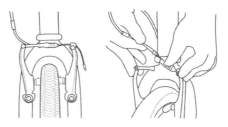

With a V-brake, squeeze the brake arms together to ease the tension so the cable can be released.

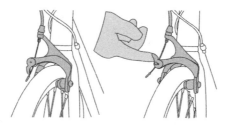

Open the quick-release lever if the brake has one.

Release the wheel from the frame next.

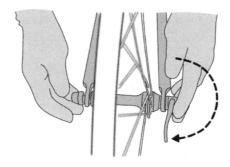

Open and hold the lever on a quick-release axle while unscrewing the nut on the opposite side.

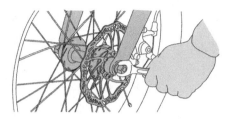

With a wrench, loosen the bolt attached to the axle.

Tip: Flipping the bike upside down or using a bike stand can help. Make sure your panniers and other bags are removed before doing this.

Follow these steps to remove the rear wheel:

Place your chain on the smallest cog of the rear cassette.

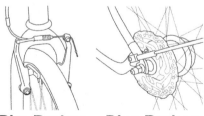

Rim Brakes   Disc Brakes

When removing the wheel, open up the rim brakes so the tire does not get stuck.

In the case of disc brakes, you will not need to release the brakes.

Quick-release axle systems are common on wheels. Loosen the lever by spinning; you might need to unscrew the nut on the other side.

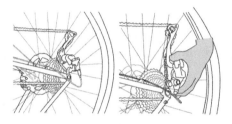

Lift the chain off the cog by pushing the rear derailleur back.

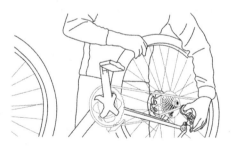

With the other hand, remove the frame's dropouts from the wheel.

Tips:

- When opening your bike's quick-release mechanism, be careful not to touch the brake rotor because it can be hot enough to burn you. Also, do not get any oil or other contaminants on your disc brakes.

- Make it a habit to take the wheel on and off frequently. You'll become more proficient at it the more often you do it.

2. *Remove The Tube*

Deflate your bike's tires completely. There are two methods for this depending on your valve.

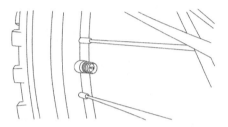

Press down on the small pin in the center of the tire valve if you have a wider Schrader valve (the type found on most car tires).

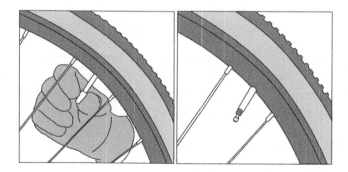

Remove the plastic dust cap from the thinner Presta valve if you have one, turn the small valve at the top counter-clockwise and press down to release the air.

To remove the tire bead (the part of the tire that fits under the rim), follow these steps:

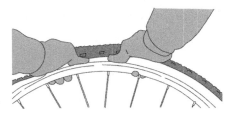

Without a tire lever, unseating the tire bead is more difficult, but you can work your way around the rim by pushing the tire bead edge toward the middle. Move the tire bead over the outside edge of the rim.

Use tire levers if you have them for additional leverage. To avoid damaging the valve stem, start using tire levers on the side that is opposite the valve. To lift the bead of the tire over the edge of the rim, use the longer end of the tire lever.

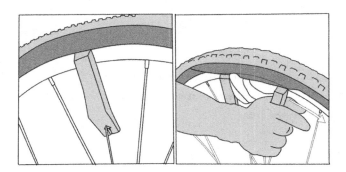

If you cannot unseat the tire with just one lever, place a second lever approximately two or three spokes to the side of the first.

A notch on tire levers can be used to secure the lever against a spoke, keeping it in place.

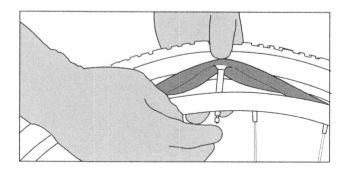

When you have freed a section of the tire bead, you should be able to free the rest of it with your fingers. After pulling the valve stem out of the rim, remove the inflatable tube from beneath the tire.

The tube should easily slide out of the rim. When pulling out the valve through the rim, be careful not to damage it on the sharp edge of the rim.

3. *Find the Cause of the Flat Tire*

Examine the tire and tube for cuts, punctures, and tears. To prevent getting another flat immediately after replacing your tube, observe the following to find the cause.

The tire: Work your way from the outside of the tire inward. Inspect the tread for embedded objects.

Using your thumb and index finger, feel the inside of the tire.

If you find anything, examine the tube in the same approximate location to see if it's damaged.

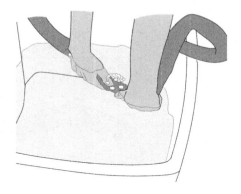

The tube: Tube damage can be difficult to detect. Check for air loss by inflating the tube if there are no obvious punctures or blowouts. You can find very small leaks by bringing the tube close to your face and feeling or listening for air, or submerging it in water and looking for bubbles.

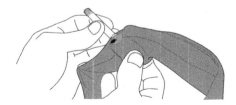

The valve: If the stem or base of the valve is cracked, cut, or severely worn, it may leak. In this case, the entire tube will need to be replaced.

The rim: Check for any protruding spoke ends or any points where the tube may be pinched against an opening for a spoke.

Tips:

- The tire should not be completely removed from the wheel. After identifying damage somewhere on your tire, rim, and/or tube, you should check the other parts of the tire, rim, and/or tube in order to determine the problem.

- Your bike repair kit should include tweezers for removing small items from your tire or tube.

4. *How To Determine If Your Tube Should Be Replaced or Repaired*

- When To Replace The Tube

When out riding, many bikers may choose to replace a damaged tube with a new one instead of repairing the old one right away.

Whenever the damage to the tube is too severe or extensive to be patched, the patch job does not hold, or when the tube's valve is damaged, you should replace the tube instead of patching it.

- How To Repair A Damaged Tube

A patching kit typically includes everything you need in order to make an effective patch in the field.

You can fix your tube in the following ways:

1. Identify the damaged area.

2. Clean the damaged area and dry it.

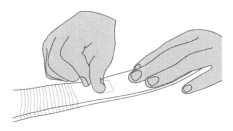

3. Use sandpaper to rough up the damaged area (so the glue sticks better).

4. The glue (vulcanizing fluid) must be spread and allowed to set until tacky.

5. Put the tube patch on and press it firmly in place.

Repair hack: Folded dollar bills (or an empty energy gel wrapper) can be used to temporarily repair a tear in a tire sidewall. It should be positioned between the tire and the tube so that it covers the gap and prevents the tube from bulging. Shoe glue can also be used.

5. *Putting A Bike Tube Into A Wheel*

1. Inflate your tube partially to ensure it holds air and gives it some shape.

2. You must push one edge (or "bead") of the tire inside the rim when your tire has been completely removed from the rim.

3. Next, put the valve stem into the valve hole on the rim. Make sure that the valve stem is straight and not angled.

4. Insert the rest of the tube into the tire.

5. Push the other tire bead into the rim by starting at a point opposite the valve.

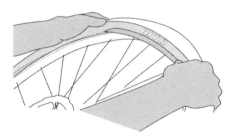

6. Make sure to work the tire bead inside the rim as you go around the wheel (in both directions at once). Eventually, it will become more difficult. To make the job easier, pinch both sides of the tire toward the rim, or use a tire lever to assist you.

Be careful when you use a tire lever to avoid pinching the tube.

7. Ensure that the tube is not caught between the rim and the tire bead after installing the tire and valve.

If this happens, you might get another flat.

8. As you inflate your tire, make sure the tire bead stays firmly seated on both sides of the rim. Make sure the valve remains straight as you inflate.

Make sure your tube does not get caught between your tire and the rim by pinching the tire on both sides inward.

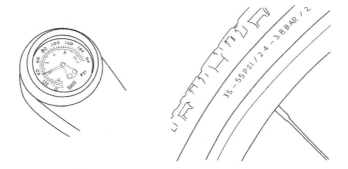

9. Make sure you inflate the tire to the recommended pressure (printed on the tire or in your owner's manual).

Use your thumb as a guide if you don't have a gauge.

Continue pumping if your thumb fits easily.

6. *Reinstalling the Wheel*

- How to Put the Rear Wheel Back On

1. Turn your bike over so that the top section of the chain hangs over the smallest cog in your cassette.
2. The axle of the wheel should line up with the dropouts on the bike frame. As you lower the axle, pull the derailleur back to get it out of the way. Make sure the axle is firmly seated in the dropouts.
3. Tighten the nut on the bike's drive side while holding the quick-release lever. Then close the lever. Don't let it touch the bike's frame. Tuck it out of the way. If the lever closes or touches the frame too easily, it may not be tight enough.
4. Don't forget to reconnect your brakes (if necessary) and make sure they are working.
5. Make sure that the gears shift smoothly when you spin the pedals.

- How to Put the Front Wheel Back On

1. The axle of the front wheel should be lined up with the dropouts in the fork, and the wheel should be lowered into position. Ensure the axle is seated in the dropouts.
2. While tightening the nut, hold the quick-release lever in place. Close the lever when the nut is tight. Be sure it's tucked out of the way and doesn't touch the bike's frame. The lever should not be able to close too easily, or it will touch the frame. Tighten the nut further if the lever is touching the frame.
3. If necessary, reconnect the brakes and ensure they're working.

Some general tips:

- Practice repairing the flat bike tire several times at home to overcome any fears you may have.
- Move away from an unsafe area if you get a flat tire there. Get off your bike and walk it to a public place.

Switching Brake Pads

The brake pads on bikes don't usually have the longest shelf life, just like those on cars. Luckily, they're so tiny that you can always keep a couple of spares in your pocket when you're out. A simple flat-head screwdriver is usually all you need to change them, and you can generally do the job yourself. Although removing the wheel can make the process easier, many riders find it's just fine with it still attached. It's up to you.

As you remove the brake pad, remember to pay attention to the orientation, then slip on the new one. If your old grub screw is still in good condition, use it. Once the new pads are installed, you'll want to lower the cable tension and adjust the alignment before you hit the road again.

You should pay attention to the specifications when buying brake pads since not all of them work with all brands.

How To Switch Brake Pads

1. *Remove The Wheel*

- For disc brakes

Remove the thru-axle from the hub by opening and unthreading it, then lower the wheel out of the dropouts. Note: Never pull the hydraulic disc brake lever without a rotor between the pads or a brake block between the pads. It can cause the pistons to pop out of the seals. This, at the very least, makes it hard to reinstall the pistons. And, at worst, it means an extensive brake service.

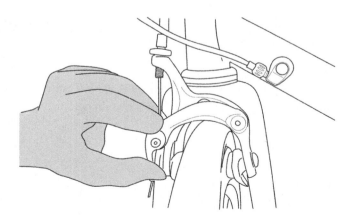

- For rim brakes

Shifting the gears to the smallest cog will make it easier for the wheel to slide past the rear derailleur cage when the rear wheel is removed and re-installed. Take off the quick-release skewer. You might need to jiggle the wheel a bit to get it out.

As you work on your front wheel, loosen the skewer nut opposite the lever just enough to pull the wheel out of the dropouts. Open the brake caliper with a small lever or button.

2. *Examine The System. (Repeat This Every Few Weeks To Ensure That It Does Not Wear Out.)*

Tools Needed: Flashlight, and Vernier calipers to measure rotor width (only disc)

- Disc

It's time to switch brake pads if there is less than one millimeter left in the brake pad material. Another sign you need to replace your brake pads is scoring or grooves on the rim or disc rotor, which indicate a gouged brake track-either from debris in the pad or from the metal shoe being worn down from the pad.

The rotors don't wear out as quickly as pads, but they eventually do. Rotors should be replaced if they are less than 1.5 millimeters thick at the brake track or if they are damaged or warped.

- Rim

Most rim brake pads include a directional indicator at the top, which is also used to let you know when the pads need to be replaced. Additionally, brake pads will have vertical slotted lines that perform the same function.

When the indicator no longer works or when the slots on the braking face of the pad no longer show, it's time for a new set.

3. *Remove The Pad Retention Bolt or Screw*

Tools Needed: Flat-head screwdriver, needle-nose pliers, or hex wrench (usually three-millimeter)

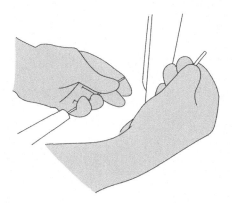

- Disc

Disk brake pads are often held in place by horizontal screws or bolts. Other systems use magnets instead. Screws are threaded into calipers and/or held in place by circlips or fixing pins. With the pliers, carefully remove the pin or circlip, then unscrew or slide the bolt.

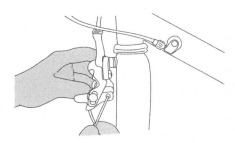

- Rim

A small set screw is often found on the side of the brake shoe. Then unthread it, but not completely-just enough so you can wiggle the pad in the shoe. For older systems, you may need to pull out a pin instead. But if there's neither, you can just slide the pad out.

Note: These are only instructions for swappable pads in systems that have separate brake shoes and pads. There are some inexpensive brakes that have one-piece pads/shoes that must be unbolted.

4. *Remove The Used Pads*

Tools Needed: Pliers, maybe.

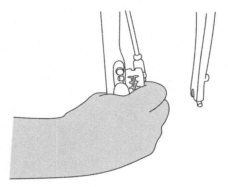

- Disc

For removing disc brake pads, they typically have a tab on the back. The pads are often set loosely in a thin metal frame; be careful not to drop them while removing the pads. Magnet-style pads do not have frames.

Grab the small tabs on the backs of the pads with fingers or pliers, squeeze them together, and firmly pull the pads – as well as the spring if applicable – out of the caliper.

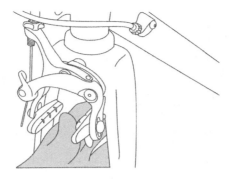

- Rim

When the set screw is sufficiently backed out for the pad to move, gently pull it out of the shoe. Remove the pads toward the rear of the bike.

5. Clean And Examine The Bike

Tools Needed: A clean rag, flashlight, rubbing alcohol, piston press or any other broad, flat tool.

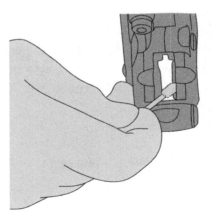

- Disc

Examine the inside of the caliper with the flashlight. There are two (or sometimes four) flattish cylinders inside, and sometimes a stubby post in the middle. These are the brake pistons, which move the brake pads back and forth. Disc brakes automatically adjust for pad wear, so repositioning the pistons might be necessary. Carefully press each piston back into the caliper body using a piston press (or any other flat, broad tool). A dirty or sticky piston might not want to re-seat, so you'll need to bleed the system (bike shops will do this for you) and clean the pistons. That's for another day, though.

Clean the brake tracks of the disc rotor with rubbing alcohol and a clean rag. Do not touch the rotor's brake track with your bare hands; the system can be contaminated by skin oils. If the rotor bolts or Centerlock attachment rings are loose, this is a good time to tighten them.

- Rim

Check the brake track on the wheel rim. There may be some foreign material in the pad if there are gouges and grooves. The pads should be swapped, but you can also wipe down the rim with rubbing alcohol and a clean rag. Watch for signs of damage such as split carbon fibers, deep gouges, or other structural damage to carbon fiber wheels. It's best to have a shop inspect the wheel if you have any concerns. For metal rims, you can gently sand out the rubber and dirt deposits with fine-grit sandpaper or a brake cleaning block, then clean it with a rag and alcohol. You will also get better braking performance.

6. Replace The Pads

Tools Needed: Pliers, and latex or any clean gloves.

Put on gloves. The skin oils will contaminate disc brake pads, which will result in noisy braking and decreased power. If applicable, unpack the new brake pads and their springs. As you slide the pads and spring them into the caliper, you will feel them seat in place, but there may not be an audible click. Replace the horizontal retention screw or bolt, as well as the fixing pin, if applicable.

Whenever you need to replace pads, be aware that they come in two different materials: resin/organic or metallic. Stick with the same material as your existing brake pads if you like the way your brakes perform.

Most bikes come with rubber/organic pads, which mix materials such as rubber, kevlar, and carbon. Although they're typically quieter and have better modulation, they wear out more quickly in wet conditions and can lose power while braking hard for long periods.

Metal, or sintered, pads have a better hold under sustained braking and won't wear out as quickly in mud, but they're noisy, don't bite as much initially, and tend to wear out rotors more quickly. Metallic brake pads are recommended if you notice excessive wear from riding in wet conditions or feel your brakes fade on long descents.

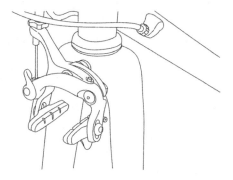

- Rim

Brake direction indicators are located on the top of the pad (lefts and rights). Gently slide the pad into the shoe. As it gets deeper into the shoe, you may need to exert more force to fully seat it. Tighten the set screw back into place to secure it.

7. Reinstall The Wheel And Bed The Rotors

Tools Needed: Possibly a tire lever or flat-blade screwdriver for disc systems.

- Disc

Putting the pistons back in place (step five) does not always work. When you reinstall the wheel, the pads may be tight around the rotor. Check to see if the pistons retract by squeezing the brake lever several times. Then spin the wheel. When the pads are still too close to the rotor, you will hear the pads brush against each other and there will not be much lever throw before the brake engages. This can be corrected by removing the wheel and inserting a flat-bladed screwdriver between the pads or a tire lever. Reinstall the pistons by re-seating each pad in the caliper body.

When you change pads, especially if you switched from organic to metallic, you should "bed-in" the rotors to the new pads. Basically, this means ensuring enough pad material is distributed evenly across the rotors so the braking will be smooth, powerful, and free of vibration. Try to pedal at 10 miles per hour on your street, then slowly increase the force of your brakes. Do not completely stop. Repeat this five to ten times on each side. Do the same process while pedaling 15 to 20 miles per hour. Your initial brake power should increase with each repetition.

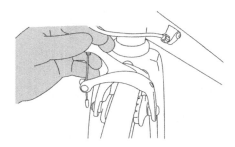

- Rim

Likewise, if your old, worn-out pads are replaced with new, full-thickness ones, you may notice that the brakes are dragging or feeling too tight. The brake caliper's quick-release should be closed so the pads can touch the rim, and the brake shoe must be properly positioned. The brake pad should contact the rim brake track, but should not extend off the bottom of the brake track or touch the tire when the brake lever is pulled. The brake pad should maintain its contact evenly from top to bottom. In fact, it's better to have the front of the pad touch the rim slightly before the rear. By doing this, you will reduce shuddering and braking noises. Check your barrel adjusters, just above the caliper, if the pad is properly aligned and the system drags. Check the brake lever throw again after two complete counterclockwise rotations. As you keep going, the pads should not drag on the rim and the lever throw should be where you want it. Even if you have fully backed off the barrel adjuster and it's still too tight, you may have to adjust the brake cable tension at the cable fixing bolt on the caliper.

PREPARATION FOR RIDING THE TRAIL

Safety starts long before you get on the bike! It is often said that a little common sense and smart thinking will go a long way toward preventing injuries. Here's what you should be careful of during the preparation phase:

- Pay attention to the weather. Look at the latest reports to see what the weather will mean for the trail.
- The strength of numbers. Avoid riding alone in remote areas. It is best to have at least two other people with you in case someone gets injured. That way, one person can seek help while the other attends to the injured.
- Additionally, fellow riders will help protect you from crime and bike theft.
- Study the trail map before you go riding, know where the challenges may be and how long you will be riding. Make sure you are prepared for steep inclines, tricky terrain, or darkness.
- Be aware of where you are and where you are going. Let your friends and family know where you will be riding and when you expect to return.
- It is a good idea to finish your ride before dusk in case you have bike troubles or if you go a little off route.
- Be sure to plan your exit routes too, so if you have problems at any point along the way, you will be able to determine the fastest and safest route to services.
- A map, compass, and/or GPS unit are more important when exploring a new trail. In case of weather changes, things may appear very different in rain or fog.
- Prepare for the worst-case scenario. Always carry a mobile phone or another type of communication device in case of an emergency. Write down the relevant emergency numbers.
- Charge your batteries or make sure you have spares.

- Make sure you have enough food, water, and equipment in case of an emergency.
- Be sure to notify those who maintain the trail and other riders about any changes or hazards that may occur.
- Emergencies can leave you stranded on the trail, so make sure you have a first aid kit, spare batteries, a light, rain gear, a reflective blanket, and the tools you need to fix your bike: pumps, wrenches, Y-socket tools, tire levers, Allen keys, multi-tools, and spare tires.

Physical Conditions and Limitations

Mountain biking combines skill, endurance, and strength.

In endurance sports, the better-conditioned competitor will always win. When in context with the Survival Fitness Plan, if you have more endurance than the person chasing you, then you will get away.

Here are some things to consider in regards to training, knowing your limits, and safety:

- Don't push yourself beyond your limits - know your body.
- Trust your instincts and think about what you are trying to accomplish.
- When you ride on trails far from civilization and try to 'carry on', the consequences can be quite severe.
- Riders who lack the fitness necessary to ride a particular trail may become fatigued, putting their safety at risk.
- It is best for a novice biker to train on less challenging and dangerous terrain or at lower speeds before taking on something more challenging - stay on smooth, flat trails with few sharp turns or steep descents.
- You should practice riding the bike in a variety of terrains, including wooded areas and hills. Don't tackle rocks, grass, or sharp turns until you're confident you can ride the bike no matter what is in front of you.

- Make sure you don't overextend yourself at first - building endurance and increasing your aerobic capacity will help you take on longer rides and practice your skills until you are more confident.
- Rocks, narrow spots, hills, and switchbacks (zigzagged trails) will be more challenging and are better for intermediate to advanced riders. It's best to be in good aerobic shape before you try these trails and have at least a few technical skills.
- If you take a knock, feel weak or light-headed, or would just like to stop for a few minutes, inform your riding companions.
- A weekend rider might not require much more than the right gear, some practice, and a good warm-up.
- Warm-up for at least 20 minutes beforehand. This increases blood flow to your muscles, making them less susceptible to injury.
- Stretch your muscles, especially your hamstrings, calves, quadriceps, neck, lower back, and shoulders.
- By exercising regularly, you will strengthen the muscles you'll use for mountain biking and gain the endurance you'll need for long rides. Train with weights and swim for recovery to stay in top biking shape.

Mountain Bike Trails and Safety

To reduce the risk of accident and injury, ride trails within your range of experience.

- Learn as much as you can about the trail you'll be riding - don't try to ride like a pro if you're not familiar with it!
- You can find information about trails that interest you by reading bike and outdoor magazines, mountain biking websites, and tour guides.
- Look for signs that indicate the skill level needed to ride a particular trail.

- Plan your ride with the help of a topographical map. Make sure you know how to read the map and select the scale that will give the most detail.
- Identify specific hazards by speaking to the locals who know the trail well.
- Stay on the trail and acquaint yourself with it by following signs and route markers.
- Make sure you're familiar with the laws that apply in your area. Ensure that you're permitted to bike on the trail if it is not specifically designed for mountain biking.
- If you are not sure if cycling is legal on a particular trail, get permission from the proper authorities before trespassing on private land.
- When you are not familiar with a trail, keep a steady pace so you can adapt easily to unanticipated obstacles and unexpected trail conditions.
- Follow the trail. Slow down when you see another person. Signal that you want to pass when you see them.
- Never hesitate to walk sections you are unfamiliar/uncomfortable with!

PROTECTIVE GEAR FOR SAFE MOUNTAIN BIKING

The Bike

Before we discuss the helmet and other protective gear, we need to take a closer look at the mountain bike.

Bikes range from easily affordable for beginners to very expensive for professionals, made from better materials like aluminum or premium-grade steel, with more accessories and customization options.

As far as safety is concerned, the bike must be an appropriate one for the rider, the type of riding to be undertaken, the type of terrain you will be riding, as well as the angle of descent.

Here's a brief summary of some mountain bike characteristics:

- A mountain bike is designed to handle rough terrain. It is heavier than a cross-country bike and easily climbs hills.
- A trail mountain bike is essentially a cross-country bike with a softer suspension for crossing larger obstacles.
- Mountain bikes also feature two types of suspension systems, which protect the bike and rider from the shocks of rough terrain.
- Full suspension bikes have both rear and front suspension. In comparison to hardtail bikes, they are significantly heavier, more comfortable, and easier to control.
- Hardtail bikes lack rear suspension but have a front suspension fork. Their lighter weight and more efficient pedaling make them better suited for off-road riding, and they are also more durable.

You should also pay attention to regular pre-ride maintenance and inspection of the mountain bike. Refer to the Mountain Bike Maintenance chapter.

The Helmet

A helmet is one of the most important pieces of safety equipment. After all, it protects your head!

But just slapping any helmet on your head is not enough. You should buy a quality one that fits correctly and ensure you wear it properly.

- Make sure your helmet fits correctly - the helmet should fit tightly so that the chinstrap serves only to prevent it from falling off, rather than holding it in place.
- The side straps of your helmet should form a V-shape around your ear, while the adjuster should be located just below the ear lobe.
- A front strap will hold the helmet in place while a back strap will prevent the helmet from falling on your eyes.
- The rear strap should be centered evenly with each of the side straps, just beneath the base of the skull.
- Weak straps can lead to a completely ill-fitted helmet if the chin strap is pulled over the ear or the back strap is pulled too low.
- While talking to your friends, your helmet should pull down a bit when you open your mouth. If it doesn't, it's too loose.

Additional Protective Gear and Clothing

Mountain bikers need protection from the elements and hazards on the trails from head to toe.

- On long rides, padded shorts, baggies or lycra will make you more comfortable.
- Check that your gear is the right size and that you're wearing it properly.
- Layer your clothing for maximum comfort in cold weather.
- Pack a waterproof jacket in case of changing weather and a reflective jersey if you're riding in the dark.

- Pads for your knees and elbows will protect you from scrapes and falls, and gloves will keep your hands warm and protect you from knocks and falls when you grip the handlebars.
- For extreme downhill rides, wear a full-face helmet, appropriate limb protection, and suitable back and torso protection.
- Choose shoes that fit your pedals' cleats if you have clipless pedals. The shoes should be comfortable, durable, and have a hard sole to make pedaling more efficient.
- To prevent blisters, wear thick cycling socks.
- The right pair of sunglasses will protect your eyes from the sun's ultraviolet rays, while also keeping out dirt, wind, insects, and branches. Go for shatterproof lenses that offer high UV protection.
- Keep water and food for energy on longer cross-country trails.
- Keep some snacks with you, such as an energy bar or some fruits to keep you fueled.
- Make sure you drink plenty of water to prevent dehydration. Get a backpack-mounted system if you don't want to constantly pick up a bottle.

Helmet

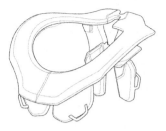

Neck brace

Goggles

Gloves

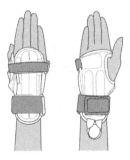

Wrist support

Protective clothing

Jacket

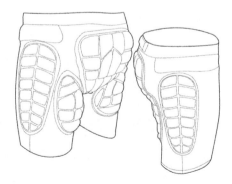

Protective shorts

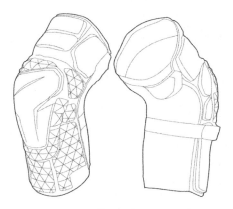

Knee pads

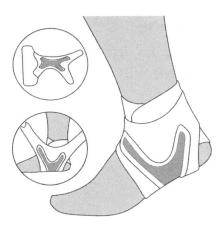

Ankle support

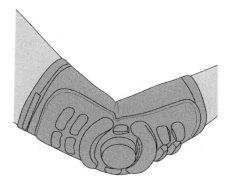

Elbow pads

MOUNTAIN BIKE SAFETY TIPS FOR BEGINNERS

Mountain biking is an exciting sport and a great way to keep fit, but it is also the most dangerous form of biking. It can lead to severe injuries, including brain trauma and even death!

Our responsibility as mountain bikers is to be as safe as possible. No matter how familiar you are with the trail or how skilled you are, you still need to follow safety procedures.

Here are some safety tips to consider:

1. Never ride without a helmet!

This is at the top of the list. This may seem obvious, but many novice riders choose to ignore it!

The single most important piece of safety equipment for mountain bikers is a high-quality, properly fitted, and well-adjusted safety helmet.

Whether it's hot, uncomfortable, or itchy, you need to wear a helmet when you're riding a bike. It really is that simple!

2. Equip yourself with the right gear

You will fall off your mountain bike as a beginner - it's part of the experience. While most of your injuries will be relatively minor, wearing the right safety equipment will help to protect you from scratches, scuffs, and scrapes that are inevitable when you do hit the ground.

Along with a helmet, you'll also want to invest in:

- A pair of gloves – to protect your hands from scrapes, cuts, and blisters

- A good pair of shoes – so you can grip the pedals well and prevent your laces from becoming entangled in the chain (another sure-fire recipe for a fall!)
- Sunglasses – to protect your eyes from the glare of the sun and from small pieces of debris while riding

Additionally, elbow and knee pads, padded shorts, body armor, and shin protection may be necessary, depending on the terrain you're planning to ride on - you'll be glad you invested in all that protection when you do fall off!

3. Understand your limits

As a new rider, it's easy to get carried away and try to tackle trails you are not good at.

When it gets tough, it is absolutely fine to get off your bike and walk - showing off and trying sections you aren't ready for can be disastrous.

Start with an easier route and build your skills before attempting challenging or dangerous trails. Be aware of any potential dangers before you attempt a trail, and even if a section seems within your capabilities, it might not be worth the risk if there is a 50ft drop to one side!

As you get tired, your skills, ability, and concentration diminish, so rest when you feel tired, and stop when you're tired.

4. Know the basics of first aid

A little first aid knowledge can save your life, so it's a very useful skill for any mountain biker. There are plenty of courses out there, as well as basic first aid books and guides online, so ignorance isn't an excuse.

Carry a small first aid kit with you on your bike. You can even find kits that attach to your bike frame, without you having to stop to use them.

5. Do a safety check on your bike

Poorly maintained mountain bikes are dangerous - make sure yours is in good shape before you ride it. One of the most important things you need to pay attention to is your brakes, since stopping quickly and safely is crucial.

Taking care of your tires, lubricating your chain (using specialized oils), and checking your mechanics for loose or broken parts is also very important. If you sense anything different while you're riding, stop and check if there's something amiss.

With some spare parts and a puncture repair kit, you can avoid being stranded with a long walk back home.

6. Be sensible

Mountain bike safety is largely a matter of common sense. When riding alone, it's important to check the weather and dress appropriately, plan your route and let your friends and family know where you're going.

If in doubt, trust your instincts; it is better to err on the side of caution rather than regret.

BASIC TECHNIQUES

It is not necessary to have mountains to go mountain biking. There is something exhilarating about being able to enjoy scenic views while biking off-pavement and exercising in the fresh air no matter what terrain you have available to you.

It takes some different skills to ride a mountain bike than to ride a road bike.

Your body position is perhaps the most important aspect of mountain biking.

You'll find rocks, roots, ruts, sand, or even mud on mountain bike trails. While it can be fun to ride on the varied terrain, the potential obstacles can be nerve-wracking to beginners.

Positioning yourself correctly will help you maneuver through tricky sections.

The two primary body positions are neutral and ready.

Neutral Position

You should always be in a neutral position on your bike when riding non-technical sections of the trail.

This position includes:

- Level and evenly weighted pedals
- Bending the knees and elbows slightly
- The index fingers on the brake levers (rim brakes generally require two fingers).
- Keep your eyes 15 to 20 feet ahead, look where you want to go rather than where you don't.

Ready Position

When the trail steepens or gets rockier, you should move into the ready position (also known as the attack position). This position gets you mentally and physically ready to tackle technical trail sections. This position includes:

- Level and evenly weighted pedals
- Knees and elbows bent deeply (imagine your arms bent 90 degrees to make chicken wings).
- Take the rear end off the seat and shift your hips back
- The back of your body is nearly parallel to the ground
- The index finger is on the brake lever 100% of the time (rim brakes generally require two fingers).
- Keep your eyes forward about 15 to 20 feet ahead; keep looking where you want to go, not where you don't.

Adjusting The Seat Position

You can get in the correct body position for climbing and descending by positioning your seat properly.

Climbing

Position your seat so that you pedal efficiently while climbing. As your foot hits the bottom of the pedal stroke, your leg should be bent a bit, reaching about 80-90 percent of its full extension. By doing so, you will be able to pedal efficiently and effectively, using the major leg muscles.

Descending

When you descend, lower your seat about two or three inches from where it was set for climbing hills. With a lower seat, you will have more control and confidence on steep descents because your center of gravity will be lower. For the most comfortable position, you may have to experiment with different seat heights.

How To Pick A Line

Beginners make the mistake of looking to avoid spots instead of focusing on where they wish to go. If you encounter difficult sections of trail, choose a path and follow it.

What are the hazards to be aware of? It depends on your skill level. For one cyclist, a log may be a barrier, but for another it can be a fun bunnyhop. Look for rock fragments, logs, wet roots, water, and other hikers, cyclists, and animals.

Check 15 - 20 feet down the trail for hazards to find your line. Next, look at your tire. Your eyes can absorb a lot of information when you do this up-and-back motion. When you are aware of hazards ahead of time, you can adjust your balance and pick a line to avoid them.

Applying Brakes

The bike slows down when you squeeze the levers. That sums it up, but learning how to brake better goes a long way to helping you feel more comfortable and secure on your bike.

How To Apply Brakes

Braking should be controlled and consistent. Most of the braking power comes from your front brake, but pulling on it too hard could send you over the bars. Do not apply heavy pressure to the brakes. Instead, apply light pressure evenly to the front and back. If you squeeze too hard or fast you are more likely to skid and lose control.

Brace yourself by moving your hips back, lowering your heels, and keeping a slight bend in your elbows and knees. Maintaining this body position on the bike prevents you from getting too far forward.

For bikes with disk brakes, hold the brake levers with your index fingers and place your other three fingers on the handlebar grips. This will give you enough control and braking power. For rim brakes, apply two fingers to the brake levers since it takes more force to engage them.

When To Apply Brakes

Brake before a turn, and then let your momentum take you through it. Then you can focus on your technique and exit the turn quickly.

You can also use momentum to get over obstacles on the trail. Many beginners slow down when approaching obstacles, but in many cases you can use momentum to navigate through the tricky sections of the trail.

How To Shift

Knowing how to shift gears properly is important because most mountain biking involves some ups and downs. When you have proper shifting habits you can power yourself more efficiently up and down hills and you will also reduce wear and tear on your bike (especially on its front cassette, chain, and rear cogs).

Shifting Often

Beginners should practice shifting gears frequently. It builds muscle memory so you can intuitively change gears without thinking about whether it's an easier or more difficult one.

Shifting Early

You shouldn't wait until you've already started up the hill to shift. Change to the gear needed before you reach steep terrain. This allows you to maintain a steady cycling cadence for maximum power. Furthermore, it prevents difficult shifting under a load that could break your chain.

When you're having trouble finding the right gear for your terrain, it's better to spin in an easier gear than to stomp in a hard gear.

You should also avoid cross-chaining. Cross-chaining is when the chain crosses awkwardly between the small chainring in the front and the small cog in the rear, or the big chainring in the front and the big cog in the rear. This occurs with both double and triple chainrings. The strain on your chain may cause it to pop off; it can also stretch it over time, shortening its life.

Lastly, never stop pedaling when you are shifting. The chain can be damaged or broken if you don't pedal as you shift.

How To Avoid Cross-chaining:

A loose chain can be annoying, but at times dangerous, so you should set up your bike correctly to minimize the risk of it happening.

When your chain starts coming off frequently when it didn't in the past, your bike setup has changed. Make sure that your drivetrain bolts are tight, that nothing has moved or gotten damaged, and that your rear wheel is correctly seated in the dropouts.

Here are some other reasons why your chain might be coming off and how to avoid it from happening.

If your chain comes off at the front

- Adjust your front derailleur limit screws

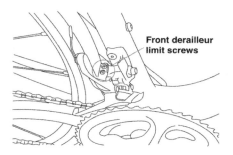

Make sure your front derailleur's two limit screws are properly adjusted if your chain is coming off the chainset.

One of the screws – sometimes marked 'H' for high, but not always – restricts the movement of the front derailleur cage.

The other screw – sometimes marked L for 'low', but not always – restricts the inward movement of the front derailleur cage.

If your chain is regularly coming off the inside of your chainset, it could be the L screw needs to be adjusted. Put the chain on the small chainring at the front, and the sprocket at the back. There should be a 1-2mm gap between the inner and outer plate of the front derailleur cage. For a larger gap, turn the L screw clockwise to bring the inner plate of the front derailleur cage closer to the chain.

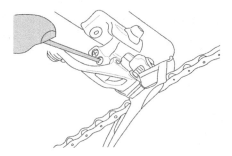

If your chain is frequently coming off the outside of your chainset, your front derailleur H screw may need to be adjusted. Put the chain on the bigger chainring (at the front) and the smallest sprocket (at the back). Derailleur cage plates shouldn't quite touch the chain on the outside. Turn the H screw clockwise if there's a gap greater than 1-2mm and you'll see the cage move in.

- Other solutions

If the limit screws are set correctly, you can still occasionally unship your chain, particularly if you change gear under load (while standing or pressing hard on the pedals). If you are shifting between chainrings, back off your effort (while still pedaling).

Another way to prevent the chain from falling off the inside of the chainset is to use a chain catcher.

The chain catcher is an arm that prevents the chain from over shifting inwards. The chain catcher is an integral part of some front derailleurs.

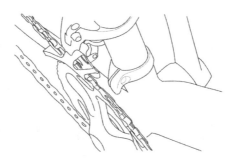

If your bike doesn't already have one, you can retrofit one. Different designs are available, and all of them are fairly easy to install.

If your chain comes off at the rear

- Adjust your rear derailleur limit screws

If your rear chain is coming off, it is often as simple as adjusting the limit screws on your rear derailleur.

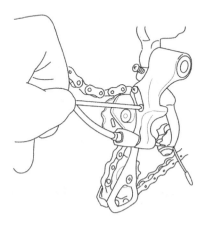

Put the chain onto the smaller chainring (at the front) and the largest sprocket (at the back) if the chain is coming off the inside of the cassette. Then turn the L screw clockwise until you can see the rear derailleur cage (the section that hangs down) moving from the center of the bike. It needs to be moved to the point where the chain can freely move into the largest sprocket, but can't go any further.

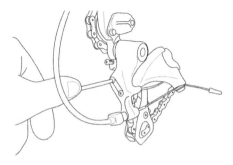

Place the chain on the larger chainring and the smallest rear sprocket if your chain is coming off the outside of the cassette. Then turn the H screw clockwise until you see the rear derailleur cage moving towards the center of the bike. You need to adjust it so that the chain can freely move into the smallest sprocket, but it cannot move beyond that.

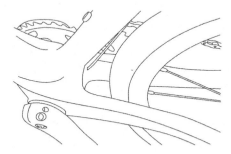

However, if the chain wasn't coming off before but has recently developed the habit, the setup must have changed. Check that the rear wheel is centered within the dropouts and that the rim is parallel to the chainstays, and check to make sure that the rear derailleur and its hanger (the part to which the rear derailleur is mounted) are not bent. The rear derailleur pulleys should be aligned directly beneath one another most of the time.

Use the stabilizer system (if you have one)

Mountain and gravel bike rear derailleurs often have stabilizing systems that keep the chain from slipping off. These systems minimize unnecessary chain movement and derailleur arm movement.

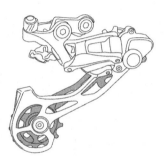

Find the on/off switch on the rear derailleur and make sure the 'on' position increases the tension if your chain jumps off often. The location varies by brand, but it's easy to find.

What if the chain still comes off?

If the chain is still coming off after doing all this, you need to look at several other factors:

- Your front derailleur may have moved.
- Is your drivetrain worn and needs to be replaced? Shifts in performance can become less smooth and more erratic as components get closer to the end of their useful lives.
- The chain might be worn, have bent or stiff links, or have become clogged with dirt. If there's a problem with the cranks, a visual inspection should reveal it.
- A chainring tooth, or the chainring itself, could be bent. A visual inspection will tell you what's wrong.

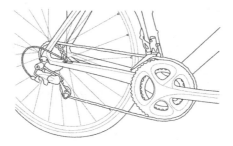

- You might be running the chain at an excessive angle - whether it be in the large chainring and the largest sprocket (pictured above), or the smaller chainring and the smallest sprocket. While some systems can handle this (even though it's not the most efficient way to ride), others can't.
- You might have a too-short or too-long chain. Thread the chain onto the largest chainring and the largest sprocket without going through the rear derailleur. Obtain the correct chain length by joining the two ends and adding one complete link (one inner and one outer half link).

- Your chain is not compatible with the rest of your drivetrain, in which case you need to replace it.
- Your drivetrain is dirty. You may not realize how much mud and gunk can affect your drivetrain. Derailleurs and chains need to run freely.

Hiking The Bike

There will always be tight spots when riding the trails. If you get stuck on a trail, don't "fight the bike." Just stay calm and try to ride it out. Seem impossible? Stop and walk it out if you have to. This is an accepted part of mountain biking. Many trails include mandatory 'hike-a-bike' sections that are too difficult for riders to handle.

Some Trail Étiquettes

A mountain biker usually rides on trails and roads that are also used by hikers and horses. Always ride courteously and responsibly and stay in control of your bike. Only ride on trails open to mountain biking. Follow these simple rules:

- Allow cyclists who are going uphill the right of way (if riding on singletrack, stop completely and lift your bike out of the trail).
- If you are approaching hikers or horses, slow down and give them a wide berth. Take direction from the horseback rider when dealing with horses.
- Be friendly to trail users - let them know you're coming.

EVASIVE RIDING TECHNIQUES

Most people know how to ride, but many do not know how to ride fast or through obstacles safely. This section will teach you how.

Basic Drills

Use the following drills to improve your basic riding skills.

Stand and Coast

Stand on your pedals without sitting on the seat and just coast. Keep your arms bent and don't lock your knees. Keep your pedals level.

Next, shift your body towards the rear of the bike. Use this position when coasting over obstacles or rough terrain.

Stand and Pedal

Lift yourself off the seat and pedal.

Track Stand

Balance the bicycle in place, keeping your feet on the pedals. Use this technique when you have to move quickly or stop short to analyze an obstacle without losing your rhythm.

Coast at a slow speed, pedals level, and then come to a stop. Find your balance position. You can stand, sit, turn your wheel at an angle, etc.—whatever works for you.

Rock back and forth lightly. To rock forward, let off the brake a little. To rock back pull the bike back underneath you. Repeat this procedure.

Keep pressure on your front pedal while holding the brake to keep you in place.

Slow Ride

Ride between two points as slowly as possible without putting your foot down. Ride forward at all times—no zigzagging, etc.

Heel Grab

The goal is to grab onto one of your heels and keep riding along normally.

Pedal normally, then lean to your left and use your left hand to grab your left heel. Continue to hold your heel as you pedal. You can start off holding your calf, then move to your ankle, then your heel.

Bottle Pick Up

Ride towards an upright bottle so it is just off to your side. As you ride past the bottle, lean over and pick it up off the ground. Next, place it back on the ground in an upright position.

Slalom

Look straight ahead and weave in and out of a set of obstacles in a zigzag fashion—that is, to the left of the first obstacle, the right of the second, the left of the third etc.

Start with the obstacles in a straight line about six feet apart and bring them closer together as you improve.

Offset Slalom

Use the same setup as with the regular slalom, but take every other cone and move it left or right by two or three feet.

You'll have to take wider, sweeping turns and lean more to get around the obstacles. Continue to look ahead.

Figure 8's

Ride your bike in figure eight in as small a space as possible without putting your foot down.

Gap Storming

Arrange two lines of cones in a V formation. Ride between them without hitting any.

As your confidence increases, move the final pair closer and closer together.

Down A Curb

Coast straight down off a curb. Absorb the drop with your arms and legs.

Advanced Skills

Fixing a Dropped Chain

If your chain drops onto the bottom bracket, just pedal easily and gently shift up with the big gears.

If the chain is jammed, get off the bike and manually put it back on.

If the chain falls outside the crank arm—on your foot, for example —then roll and shift down toward the small ring. You can use your foot to help place it back on.

Learning to Crash

Most people won't like falling off their bikes, but if you're mountain biking, it'll probably happen at some point.

Try to keep your arms in when you fall off your bike. Instinctively, you may reach out to brace your fall, but this can cause a broken wrist or collarbone.

Instead, learn to roll. Once you know the basic roll, get comfortable doing a forward roll after a running dive. Finally, progress to "crash" rolling after slamming on your front brakes when riding on grass.

The most common damage after a fall is to your pride. Pick yourself up, dust yourself off, and check that you are not injured. After that, check your bike. Maybe the seat or handlebar twisted, or maybe the chain came off.

How to Roll

Here is a rolling tutorial from the "Essential Parkour Training" training manual.

Choose which side you are most comfortable rolling over, right or left. Eventually, you'll want to learn to roll on both sides.

If rolling over your left shoulder, start from a kneeling position with your left foot forward.

Place your hands on the ground in front of you, so that your thumbs and index fingers form a kind of diamond shape. Put them at a 45° angle in the direction that you want to roll in.

Note: You could just roll over your shoulder, but unless you have something in your hands it's preferable to use them to help control your motion, as well as to absorb some of the impacts.

Look over your right shoulder and use your rear leg to push you over into the roll. Use your hands to control your momentum and your arms to lift you a little, so that you can land on the back of your shoulder blade. You do not want to hit on the top of your shoulder.

Roll diagonally across your back to your opposite hip. If you roll wrong (which you probably will when first learning), you'll feel it. When you start practicing on hard surfaces, you will definitely know if you're rolling poorly. It's a learning curve.

Come up from your roll between your tail and hip bones, and use the side of your leg and your momentum to get back onto your feet.

You could also come straight up onto your feet instead of using your thigh. This will save your knee from contacting the ground, but puts more pressure on your ankle as you stand.

As you get more confident, start from taller positions such as squatting and standing. A good exercise is to stand straight and let your body fall forward like a plank.

At the last moment, roll out of it. This can be done with side and back rolls as well.

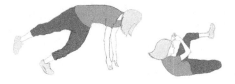

Progress to rolling with momentum and with jumps.

When jumping into a roll, be sure to keep your legs flexed as you land and allow the momentum to push you into the roll.

Eventually, you will be able to jump and roll from ledges. It is important to slowly work your way up and increase the strength in your legs so that you can do bigger and bigger drops.

As the height and speed of your drops increase, it will help to land with your feet closer together and to be more adaptable with your arms.

Cornering

Always look where you want to go. Anticipate the speed for the corner and brake before the corner if necessary. Never brake while turning. Approach the corner wide.

Cut to the apex (the straightest line through a corner), and finish wide.

If you stop pedaling, put all your weight onto the outside pedal so it faces down towards the road. Resume peddling as soon as you have passed the apex.

Riding Faster

Push and pull the pedal around as if keeping the pedal to the outside of the circle.

Lift your knees faster and higher.

Riding Uphill

If you need to shift during a climb, take a couple of power strokes first. Soft pedal for a stroke while you shift, then pedal hard again.

On the road, you can stand, but on dirt, stay seated.

Slide your bum forward on your seat, and lean over the handlebars. Put your elbows back (not down). Pedal smoothly.

Riding Downhill

To prevent the chain from falling off, shift into the big chainring.

Stand with pedals level and shift your weight over the back wheel. Stay loose on the bike. Don't lock your elbows or clench your grip. Steer with your body. Let your shoulders guide you.

Brake on solid dirt or rock where you can get traction, as opposed to on loose soil or gravel.

Floating Over Terrain

On rough terrain, let the bike float underneath you. It will move in different directions as it hits bumps. Keep your body upright and the bike pointed down the trail.

Looking Behind

Make sure the path ahead is clear. Relax your right arm to drop your shoulder a little. Your elbow should bend and your right hand should be relaxed. Turn your head left and slide your butt to the right as you glance over your shoulder.

Down A Ledge

Shift your weight back, drop your wrists to pull up the handlebars, and level the bike. Shift your weight forward as the rear wheel goes airborne.

Log Hopping

Get in the same position as if you were riding downhill.

Front Pull

Coast at medium speed and, without braking, push down on the handlebars. Pull upward and straighten your arms to bring the front wheel off the ground. Place it back down gently.

Hip-Hop

Shift your weight forward and turn your pedals so that your feet are almost vertical. Press back against the pedals as you push your legs up. Pull the back end up with your leg muscles, then bring it down gently.

Log Hopping

When you are log-hopping, the front pull and hip-hop become one motion. Perform the front pull and bring the wheel high enough to clear the log. Touch the front wheel on top of the log and, as the wheel starts to roll over it, do hip-hop. If the log is wet, avoid touching your wheels on the top of it to prevent slipping.

Bunny Hopping

A bunny-hop is similar to a log-hop, but with the intention of having both wheels off the ground at the same time.

Perform a front pull and while your front wheel is in the air, use the push/pull motion to get the back wheel up. Level your bike in the air and try to squeeze your legs together. Land your back wheel first.

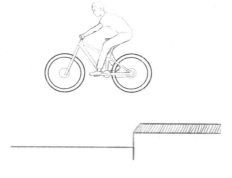

FIRST AID AND INJURY PREVENTION TIPS

Mountain biking is an extreme sport and accidents can (and will) happen. When they do occur, either to yourself or your riding partners, you need to know how to act and who to contact.

Here are a few things you should know before riding your bike. This is not intended to scare you off biking. Many of these tips are common sense! But we all need a reminder now and then.

Before Heading Out

- Make sure you have the number of your local police or emergency service on hand. If you don't like riding with a phone, take a ride with someone who does, so that you can call for help if an accident occurs.
- Make sure someone knows where you are going and how long you are going to be out (especially if you are going on a trail ride).
- Pack a first aid kit and know how to use it (this is especially important if you're going for a trail ride).

Prevent Getting Injured

- Protect yourself with a helmet, elbow pads, knee pads, back protectors, and safety jackets. They are for your protection.
- Don't ride tracks that are too difficult for you. Sadly, riding above your level of skill and others putting pressure on you is one of the most common causes of park accidents.
- Don't go too fast. For an MTBer, this is the hardest thing ever - you want to push yourself just enough to become better and faster, but you also want to keep yourself safe.
- Check the track beforehand. Make sure you are familiar with the technical sections and big features. If you think

you "know" a track, double-check. It can change in a few days, even overnight.

- In case of injury, slow down and stop. If you see an obstacle on the trail, such as an upside-down bike, stop sign, quad, person waving, etc., it suggests there has been an accident further along the trail. Stop, ensure the injured person is being taken care of, and then push your bike around.

In Case Of An Accident

- The trail should be closed. It is important to close the trail after an accident (especially on busy bike trails or in bike parks). Stop people from falling down the trail by getting someone to stand higher up. If you're riding down a feature, fast section, or blind corner, make sure that the trail is closed off so that the riders coming down can see you clearly.
- Contact bike patrol or emergency services. The bike patrol can help you if you sustain a serious injury and you are in a bike park. Call the emergency services if you are riding a trail through the forest.
- Perform first aid (if you know how). Care for and monitor the injured person as best as you can until help arrives.

First Aid For The Trail

To help stabilize the victim before medical staff arrives, many emergencies must be dealt with immediately.

Here are some common bike injuries and how to treat them. On top of those listed, there are many other serious injuries that can occur on the trail. Learn how to treat a broader range of injuries by taking a first aid course.

Lacerations

Make sure that the wound is thoroughly cleaned. Clear any debris from the wound with a gentle spray of clean water from a water bottle. Never touch or cover the wound with soiled materials. Put a sterile dressing on the wound if possible. You can also use a clean, dry piece of clothing.

To stop bleeding from severe cuts, apply pressure. To stop steady bleeding, put pressure on the wound directly with a cloth or hand.

To slow bleeding, the sides of the wound may also need to be pushed together. Where there is arterial bleeding, it is necessary to apply pressure directly to the artery near the wound. To reduce the bleeding, elevate the wound above the heart as high as possible.

Broken Collarbone

This is a common injury that many riders have experienced. Use a shirt to create a sling to secure the arm that is on the same side as the break.

Position the arm at a 90-degree angle. If you have safety pins, you can pin the bottom of the rider's own shirt to the chest of his shirt as he pulls up his arm.

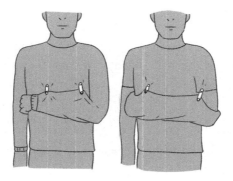

Broken Arm, Wrist, or Leg

Put a splint on the area from above the broken area to below it. Make the splint from lightweight but strong materials. Sticks, flat pieces of wood, or even a bike-mounted pump could be used. To secure the splint, you can wrap clothing or an inner tube around it.

For a broken wrist or forearm, in addition to the splint, also make a sling. If it's an upper-arm break, make a sling that only wraps around the neck and wrist.

Broken Finger

Make a splint by taping the broken finger to another finger. Put something soft between the fingers to make it more comfortable, for example, a piece of clothing.

Concussion

Riders can sustain a concussion even if they don't lose consciousness. With head injuries, it's always best to be cautious. Just walk your bikes until you can get help, and don't allow the rider to get back on the bike.

Keep an eye on the rider's condition. Vomiting, headaches that worsen with time, becoming less alert or less conscious, and bruising behind the ear or around the eyes can all be signs of concern.

To learn more about first aid visit: https://www.sfnonfictionbooks. com/wilderness-travel-medicine

CONCLUSION

It is hard to imagine a more amazing hobby than mountain biking, especially if you prefer to ride over rough terrain at high speed. It involves special bikes that are made from durable materials and can be maneuvered across a variety of terrains with ease. Mountain biking can be broken down into various categories: cross country, downhill, urban/street, dirt jumping, free riding, and all-mountain biking.

1. It's accessible

Mountain biking is a great exercise that requires no experience or membership in a gym. All you have to do is put on your biking gear and head out. Another advantage is that most places have different terrains. While you live in the city, you still have access to many terrains a short drive away. All you have to do is get ready and head out.

2. You can spend quality time with family and friends

It is one of the best ways to spend time with those you love. Bike riding is a great way to unite and get people talking, and it is great for people of all ages. This is a wonderful way for families and friends to interact.

3. You can lose yourself in nature

We are surrounded by many gadgets that keep us busy at home, such as smartphones, tablets, personal computers, and laptops. However, it's important to refrain from technology and return to the basics. Mountain biking does not depend on these gadgets, but rather on terrains and gears. It is more engaging and appealing compared to technology because it is similar to hiking. You can learn different things when you are away from home. There is nothing like the beauty of nature.

4. It is an excellent exercise

There is no end to the variety of exercise programs that are available to shape and strengthen your body. Each exercise program has its own unique effects and benefits. Simple exercises can provide plenty of benefits. Biking is an excellent form of exercise, and you do not need any prior training.

5. It is calming and relaxing

Life is full of ups and downs, and we must make every effort to meet all our needs. The stress of everyday life may sometimes make us feel down. Biking is one of the best ways to reduce stress and improve your health. Mountain biking has numerous benefits. First of all, fresh air will recharge your lungs. Second, spending some time outside helps you to relax and appreciate nature.

Ultimately, mountain biking is extremely beneficial for the mind, the body, and the soul. It is simple and does not require any training. You are exposed to new experiences and environments. This provides an excellent opportunity for friends and family to get together and spend quality time together. It would be a great experience for you to be out of your home. So what are you waiting for? Grab your bike and gear and head out for an adventure!

THANKS FOR READING

Dear reader,

Thank you for reading *A Complete Introduction to Mountain Biking*.

If you enjoyed this book, please leave a review where you bought it. It helps more than most people think.

Don't forget your FREE book chapters!

You will also be among the first to know of FREE review copies, discount offers, bonus content, and more.

Go to:

https://www.SFNonfictionBooks.com/Free-Chapters

Thanks again for your support.

REFERENCES

Andrews, G. (2013). *Complete mountain bike maintenance.* Bloomsbury Sport.

Ansari, M., Nourian, R., & Khodaee, M. (2017). Mountain Biking Injuries. *Current Sports Medicine Reports, 16*(6), 404–412. https://doi.org/10.1249/jsr.0000000000000429

Bicycle Warehouse. (2020, December 17). *Top Five Mountain Bike Maintenance Tips.* Bicycle Warehouse. https://bicyclewarehouse.com/blogs/news/top-five-mountain-bike-maintenance-tips

Chaudhry, S. (2001). Mountain biking can be dangerous. *BMJ, 323*(Suppl S1), 0107224a. https://doi.org/10.1136/sbmj.0107224a

Foster, P. (2018, December 11). *How to Adjust the Chain Tension on a Mountain Bike.* SportsRec. https://www.sportsrec.com/7933383/how-to-adjust-the-chain-tension-on-a-mountain-bike

Global Mountain Bike Network. (2019a, May 29). *Basics With Blake | Core Mountain Bike Skills.* Www.youtube.com. https://www.youtube.com/watch?v=eLLQodRLa4Q

Global Mountain Bike Network. (2019b, August 29). *10 MTB Tips For Beginners | Setup And Riding.* Www.youtube.com. https://www.youtube.com/watch?v=T-aeFsFHmuo

Heiden Orthopedics. (2020, August 31). *Common Mountain Biking Injuries: Stats & Info.* Heiden Orthopedics. https://heidenortho.com/mountain-biking-injuries/

Humphries, D. (n.d.). *Top 10 most common mountain bike injuries and tips to avoid them | DIY Mountain Bike.* Https://Www.diymountainbike.com/. https://www.diymountainbike.com/mountain-bike-injuries/

Impellizzeri, F. M., & Marcora, S. M. (2007). The Physiology of Mountain Biking. *Sports Medicine, 37*(1), 59–71. https://doi.org/10.2165/00007256-200737010-00005

Jahnke, T. (1999). Gearing up for mountain biking. *Teaching Mathematics and Its Applications, 18*(2), 78–84. https://doi.org/10.1093/teamat/18.2.78

James. (n.d.). *How Tight Should A Bike Chain Be? - Mountainbiketrailsnearme*. Mountainbiketrailsnearme.com. Retrieved April 3, 2022, from https://mountainbiketrailsnearme.com/bike-maintenance/how-tight-should-a-bike-chain-be/#:~:text=To%20check%20the%20correct%20chain

Kelley, K. C. (2004). *Mountain biking*. G. Stevens.

Mancinelli, D. (2021, July 2). *The Complete Guide To DIY Bike Repair And Maintenance*. Tracks Less Travelled. https://trackslesstravelled.com/diy-bike-repair-and-maintenance/

MarcS. (2012, May 17). *Emergency Prep for Mountain Biking*. Singletracks Mountain Bike News. https://www.singletracks.com/mtb-gear/emergency-prep-for-mountain-biking/

Mowgliii. (2022, January 15). *Introduction to Mountain Biking for Beginners - How To Start Mountain Biking - 360Guide*. Https://360guide.info/. https://360guide.info/mtb/introduction-to-mountain-biking-for-beginners-how-to-start-mountain-biking.html#How_to_Set_Up_Your_Mountain_Bike_Before_the_First_Ride_and_What_Else_Do_You_Need

Parra, M. (2018, September 3). *What is Mountain Biking? Equipment, Types, Top Spots*. Explore-Share.com. https://www.explore-share.com/blog/mountain-biking-equipment-best-season-top-spots/

Patricio, S. (2009, January 22). *13-Point Mountain Bike Maintenance Checklist*. Singletracks Mountain Bike News. https://www.singletracks.com/mtb-gear/13-point-mtb-maintenance-checklist/

Pegasus. (n.d.). *Everything You Need to Know About Mountain Biking*. Www.flypgs.com. Retrieved April 3, 2022, from https://www.flypgs.com/en/extreme-sports/mountain-biking

REI Staff. (2019, July 9). *How to Choose a Mountain Bike*. REI; REI. https://www.rei.com/learn/expert-advice/mountain-bike.html

Richards, B. (2000). *Mountain biking*. Aladdin/Watts.

River Traditions. (n.d.). *DIY Mountain Bike Maintenance Schedule Guide | DIY Mountain Bike*. Https://Www.diymountainbike.com/. Retrieved April 3, 2022, from https://www.diymountainbike.com/diy-mountain-bike-maintenance-schedule/

Rohan. (2021, August 22). *Ultimate Mountain Bike Maintenance Checklist For 2022*. Biking Know How. https://bikingknowhow.com/mountain-bike-maintenance-checklist/

Rome, D. (2016, January 28). *Beginner mountain bike setup and maintenance tips*. BikeRadar. https://www.bikeradar.com/features/beginner-mountain-bike-setup-and-maintenance-tips/

Skills With Phil. (2019, June 29). *Tips for Beginner Mountain Bikers*. Www.youtube.com. https://www.youtube.com/watch?v=n_17-Tvjx2I

Turnbull, S. (2015). *Mountain biking*. Smart Apple Media, An Imprint Of Black Rabbit Books.

Uttley, C. (2009, October 5). *What are mountain biking categories?* HowStuffWorks. https://adventure.howstuffworks.com/outdoor-activities/biking/mountain-biking-categories.htm

Wood, T., & Fairclough, C. (1989). *Mountain biking*. F. Watts.

Zinn, L., & Telander, T. (2018). *Zinn & the art of mountain bike maintenance : the world's best-selling guide to mountain bike repair*. Velopress.

AUTHOR RECOMMENDATIONS

Teach Yourself Escape and Evasion Tactics!

Discover the skills you need to evade and escape capture, because you never know when they will save your life.

Get it now.

www.SFNonfictionBooks.com/Evading-Escaping-Capture

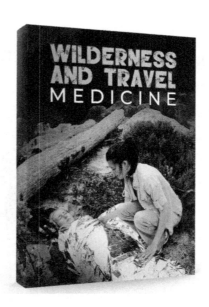

This is the Only Wilderness Medicine Book You Need

Discover what you need to heal yourself, because a little knowledge goes a long way.

Get it now.

www.SFNonfictionBooks.com/Wilderness-Travel-Medicine

ABOUT SAM FURY

Sam Fury has had a passion for survival, evasion, resistance, and escape (SERE) training since he was a young boy growing up in Australia.

This led him to years of training and career experience in related subjects, including martial arts, military training, survival skills, outdoor sports, and sustainable living.

These days, Sam spends his time refining existing skills, gaining new skills, and sharing what he learns via the Survival Fitness Plan website.

www.SurvivalFitnessPlan.com

Made in the USA
Columbia, SC
13 April 2023

15333241R00065